FISHERMAN
BIBLE STUDYGUIDES

Proverbs & Parables

God's Wisdom for Living

DEE BRESTIN

SHAW BOOKS

an imprint of WATERBROOK PRESS

Proverbs and Parables

A SHAW BOOK

PUBLISHED BY WATERBROOK PRESS

2375 Telstar Drive, Suite 160

Colorado Springs, Colorado 80920

A division of Random House, Inc.

ISBN 0-87788-694-6

Printed in the United States of America

2003

10 9 8 7 6 5 4

Contents

How to Use This Studyguide

isherman studyguides are based on the inductive approach to Bible study. Inductive study is discovery study; we discover what the Bible says as we ask questions about its content and search for answers. This is quite different from the process in which a teacher *tells* a group *about* the Bible—what it means and what to do about it. In inductive study, God speaks directly to each of us through his Word.

A group functions best when a leader keeps the discussion on target, but the leader is neither the teacher nor the "answer person." A leader's responsibility is to *ask*—not *tell*. The answers come from the text itself as group members examine, discuss, and think together about the passage.

There are four kinds of questions in each study. The first is an *approach question.* Asked and answered before the Bible passage is read, this question breaks the ice and helps you start thinking about the topic of the Bible study. It begins to reveal where thoughts and feelings need to be transformed by Scripture.

Some of the earlier questions in each study are *observation questions*—who, what, where, when, and how—designed to help you learn some basic facts about the passage of Scripture.

Once you know what the Bible says, you need to ask, *What does it mean?* These *interpretation questions* help you discover the writer's basic message.

Next come *application questions*, which ask, *What does it mean to me?* They challenge you to live out the Scripture's life-transforming message.

Fisherman studyguides provide spaces between questions for jotting down responses as well as any related questions you would like to raise in the group. Each group member should have a copy of the studyguide and may take a turn in leading the group.

A group should use any accurate, modern translation of the Bible such as the *New International Version,* the *New American Standard Bible,* the *New Living Translation,* the *New Revised Standard Version,* the *New Jerusalem Bible,* or the *Good News Bible.* (Other translations or paraphrases of the Bible may be referred to when additional help is needed.) Bible commentaries should not be brought to a Bible study because they tend to dampen discussion and keep people from thinking for themselves.

Suggestions for Group Leaders

1. Thoroughly read and study the Bible passage before the meeting. Get a firm grasp on its themes and begin applying its teachings for yourself. Pray that the Holy Spirit will "guide you into all truth" (John 16:13) so that your leadership will guide others.

2. If any of the studyguide's questions seem ambiguous or unnatural to you, rephrase them, feeling free to add others that seem necessary to bring out the meaning of a verse.

3. Begin (and end) the study promptly. Start by asking someone to pray that every participant will both understand the passage and be open to its transforming power. Remember, the Holy Spirit is the teacher, not you!

4. Ask for volunteers to read the passages aloud.

5. As you ask the studyguide's questions in sequence, encourage everyone to participate in the discussion. If some are silent, try gently suggesting, "Let's have an answer from someone who hasn't spoken up yet."

6. If a question comes up that you can't answer, don't be afraid to admit that you're baffled. Assign the topic as a research project for someone to report on next week, or say, "I'll do some studying and let you know what I find out."

7. Keep the discussion moving, but be sure it stays focused. Though a certain number of tangents are inevitable, you'll want to quickly bring the discussion back to the topic at hand. Also, learn to pace the discussion so that you finish the lesson in the time allotted.

8. Don't be afraid of silences; some questions take time to answer, and some people need time to gather courage to speak. If silence persists, rephrase your question, but resist the temptation to answer it yourself.

9. If someone comes up with an answer that is clearly illogical or unbiblical, ask for further clarification: "What verse suggests that to you?"

10. Discourage overuse of cross references. Learn all you can from the passage at hand, while selectively incorporating a few important references suggested in the studyguide.

11. Some questions are marked with a ✎. This indicates that further information is available in the Leader's Notes at the back of the guide.

12. For further information on getting a new Bible study group started and keeping it functioning effectively, read *You Can Start a Bible Study Group* by Gladys Hunt and *Pilgrims in Progress: Growing Through Groups* by Jim and Carol Plueddemann. (Both books are available from Shaw Books).

SUGGESTIONS FOR GROUP MEMBERS

1. Learn and apply the following ground rules for effective Bible study. (If new members join the group later, review these guidelines with the whole group.)

2. Remember that your goal is to learn all that you can *from the Bible passage being studied.* Let it speak for itself without using Bible commentaries or other Bible passages. There is more than enough in each assigned passage to keep your group productively occupied for one session. Sticking to the passage saves the group from insecurity ("I don't have the right reference books—or the time to read anything else.") and confusion ("Where did *that* come from? I thought we were studying _____.").

3. Avoid the temptation to bring up those fascinating tangents that don't really grow out of the passage you are discussing. If the topic is of common interest, you can bring it up later in informal conversation after the study. Meanwhile, help one another stick to the subject.

4. Encourage one another to participate. People remember best what they discover and verbalize for

themselves. Some people are naturally shy, while others may be afraid of making a mistake. If your discussion is free and friendly and you show real interest in what other group members think and feel, the quieter ones will be more likely to speak up. Remember, the more people involved in a discussion, the richer it will be.

5. Guard yourself from answering too many questions or talking too much. Give others a chance to share their ideas. If you are one who participates easily, discipline yourself by counting to ten before you open your mouth.

6. Make personal, honest applications and commit yourself to letting God's Word change you.

God's Wisdom for Living

T he book of Proverbs begins with a list of the benefits of studying "proverbs and parables" (Proverbs 1:6). This verse inspired me to interweave the themes of Proverbs with the parables of Jesus. What an adventure! The same Holy Spirit who prompted Solomon to tell "riddles" inspired Jesus to tell "stories." In fact, many of the messages in the parables of Jesus had been available to his Jewish listeners for years. They came from the book of Proverbs! The principles of God are unchanging, and it's tremendously encouraging to see the consistency of God's wisdom. Yet there are some wonderful differences between proverbs and parables that make studying them together even more beautiful and powerful than studying them separately.

Proverbs	*Parables*
• speak to our minds	• tunnel down to our hearts
• emphasize earthly life	• emphasize heavenly life
• are short, pithy	• are detailed, illustrated
• provide clarity, which encourages beginning students	• provide depth, which challenges advanced students

To avoid misinterpreting proverbs and parables, it will help to keep two principles in mind:

1. Remember that proverbs are general truths rather than promises. *Proverb* means "maxim," or general truth. You may find exceptions to the proverb, but that does not disprove the general truth. For example, Solomon repeatedly warned that laziness and poverty go hand in hand. You may find a lazy man who is rich and a hard worker who is poor, but usually this is not the case.

2. In parables, look for the central point. Jesus is giving heart and life to a principle by illustrating it with a story. You may not find every detail of a parable meaningful, and you may be led astray if you try to force it.

It is only necessary to read portions from the chapters in Proverbs for each study, but if you wish to read all of the proverbs outside of actual group time, here is one possible approach:

Day 1: Read the parable thoughtfully.

Day 2: Answer the study questions.

Day 3: Read the first proverb chapter thoughtfully. (Read either the selected proverbs or the chapter in its entirety.)

Day 4: Answer the study questions for the first proverb.

Day 5: Read the second proverb chapter thoughtfully. (Read either the selected proverbs or the chapter in its entirety.)

Day 6: Answer the study questions for the second proverb.

Day 7: Complete the study.

May the Lord be with you as you study his proverbs and parables!

Let the Wise Listen

MATTHEW 7:24-27; SELECTIONS FROM PROVERBS 1 AND 2

When playing a new board game or putting together a child's toy, I often plunge in without reading the instructions. Soon I am frustrated and must start over—with the instructions! Or I play a game a bit wrong my whole life, missing much of the game's original design.

Life is like that, but the consequences of neglecting our Creator's instructions are far more serious. Throughout Proverbs you will find the fool contrasted with the wise person. The fool lives life without fear of or regard for God, plunging in, doing things his or her own way, and reaping the consequences. In contrast the wise person listens carefully to God, obeys, and reaps the benefits. Jesus teaches the same truth in his parable of the wise and foolish builders.

1. Describe a time you forged ahead without paying attention to directions and later regretted it. What happened as a consequence?

READ MATTHEW 7:24-27.

2. To whom does Jesus compare the man who built his house on a rock? the man who built his house on the sand?

3. What is the central point of this parable?

4. Think of some specific ways that you can build your life on the Lord Jesus Christ. What can you do to show obedience, rather than complacency, in response to his words?

Read Proverbs 1:7-9,23-27.

🔥 5. Where does wisdom begin? What is a fool's response to God's wisdom and instruction (verses 7-9)?

6. What blessing is offered to the person who accepts God's rebuke (verse 23)? Have you experienced this? Explain.

7. Solomon said that the complacency of fools will kill them (Proverbs 1:32). How does he illustrate this point in verses 24-27?

READ PROVERBS 2:1-11.

8. To whom will God give wisdom (verses 1-5)? What concrete things can you do to receive this gift?

9. What are some of the benefits of seeking God's wisdom (verses 7-11)?

    Which of these benefits do you need most in your life? Why?

Along Straight Paths

LUKE 15:11-32; SELECTIONS FROM PROVERBS 3 AND 4

W e all know the story of Little Red Riding Hood. A young girl disregards her mother's warning, "Don't go off the path," and gets herself and her grandmother into a whole lot of trouble. How often we let something distract us from our goal that ends up costing us more than we'd like to pay!

A path is a metaphor for the choices we make in life. As you study these proverbs and this famous parable, consider the choices you have to make, and thank God for his direction— as well as his forgiveness when you take the wrong path.

1. Describe a time when you felt God nudging you to do something you normally wouldn't do. Did the experience end up being the right path for you? Explain.

READ LUKE 15:11-32.

2. Who does each of the sons represent? With which
    son can you most identify? Why?

3. In what specific ways is God like the father in this
    story?

4. Describe the process the wayward son had to go
    through before he could be restored to his family.

    What principles does this parable illustrate that
    would be beneficial to remember?

5. Think about the path you are on right now. In what ways are you headed straight toward God the Father? In what ways are you following your own path?

READ PROVERBS 3:5-8.

6. What are some specific things you can do to apply verses 5-6 to your life?

7. What three things do you need to do in order to stay on the right path (verse 7)?

8. Give an example of how fearing the Lord and shunning evil bring us health.

READ PROVERBS 4:3-6,10-27.

9. Compare the paths of the wicked and the righteous. What are some signs that indicate you are on the right or wrong path?

10. According to verses 14-17, how do we put ourselves "on the path of the wicked"? Aside from activities that put us on the wrong path, what information do we take in that contaminates the heart or leads us to a place we shouldn't be (verse 23)?

This week, examine your own attitudes toward instruction, discipline, and authority. Ask God to give you his wisdom and a deeper desire to follow him.

Fire in His Lap

2 SAMUEL 12:1-25; SELECTIONS
FROM PROVERBS 5, 6, AND 7

One of Aesop's fables teaches, "It is with our passions as it is with fire and water; they are good servants, but bad masters." The Bible uses fire to symbolize both good and bad. Tongues of fire rested gloriously upon the heads of Christ's followers at Pentecost, yet hell is filled with fire and brimstone.

In the book of Proverbs, fire is often used as a symbol for the passions of sex. The sayings in this study will teach us a wise approach to dealing with that fire. We'll also examine how King David, forgetting his rightful Master, was burned by the fire of his own passions—and how God forgave and healed him.

1. Describe a time when you let something monopolize your life—even a good thing. What circumstances led to your faulty priorities?

Read 2 Samuel 12:1-25.

2. In this parable, who does each of the following represent:

the rich man

the poor man

the little ewe lamb

3. What was the central point of Nathan's parable?

🖉 4. Why do you think the Lord told Nathan to confront David with a parable rather than with a direct accusation?

5. Why was the Lord's judgment against David so harsh?

6. According to verse 13, what was David's response when he was confronted with his sin?

Read Proverbs 5.

🖉 7. Some people believe that sex is wrong. How would you summarize God's view of sex as described in this passage?

What two ways of life are compared here?

8. What warnings are we given in verses 21-23?

READ PROVERBS 6:23–7:5.

9. What do the questions posed in 6:27-28 tell us about sin?

Give some examples that illustrate getting "burned."

10. Explain in your own words the concepts described in verses 30-35.

To what other sins besides adultery could these concepts apply?

11. How would obeying the commands in 7:1-5 protect a person from sexual sin?

David wrote Psalm 51 after the episode in his life described in 2 Samuel. This week, read through this psalm, applying its words to yourself and your own failures.

Come, Eat My Food

LUKE 14:15-24; SELECTIONS FROM PROVERBS 8 AND 9

O ne cold January evening we were planning to take our family and a young friend to a Christian concert. As I looked out at the blowing snow, I wished I could stay inside by the fire. I even contemplated suggesting we play Trivial Pursuit instead! But we went—reluctantly.

At that concert our young friend put her trust in Christ. As I've watched her grow over the years, I am so thankful we didn't choose Trivial Pursuit over the concert. Not only is she being saved from the snares of sin, but she is also experiencing an abundant life and is anticipating eternal life with Christ.

In this study the call of God is illustrated as an invitation to a banquet. Competing invitations, however, beckon us persuasively.

1. Can you remember a time in your life when a choice you made had a lasting impact on you or someone else? What happened?

READ LUKE 14:15-24.

2. What happened in this parable?

What impresses you? Why?

3. What excuses did those who refused the invitation give?

What comparable reasons do people give today for refusing Jesus' invitation?

4. What social class was more responsive to God's invitation? What warning or wisdom does this give you?

READ PROVERBS 8:1-21.

5. To whom is the voice of Wisdom calling in this passage?

6. What are some of the benefits of accepting Wisdom's invitation?

✐ 7. The allure of material wealth competes strongly with the call of God. What does Solomon, who experienced great material wealth as well as godly wisdom, tell us in verses 11 and 19?

How can we determine if we really value godly wisdom more than material wealth?

READ PROVERBS 9.

8. Compare the invitations of Wisdom (verses 1-6) and Folly (verses 13-18).

9. Compare the responses of the mocker/wicked and the wise/righteous in verses 8-12.

10. How do the responses of the wise and foolish in these proverbs compare to those of the banquet guests in Jesus' parable?

11. List one principle from these examples that you can apply in your own life this week.

Wealth Is Worthless

LUKE 16:19-31; SELECTIONS FROM PROVERBS 10 AND 11

E very Christmas we are reminded of Ebeneezer Scrooge. Will we hoard our hard-earned gold so we can live in comfort throughout our retirement (humbug!) years? Will we miss the joy of sharing? Will our future hold a friendless funeral? Will we be haunted one day by our stinginess on earth?

Solomon, who experienced wealth firsthand, wrote many proverbs that warn about loving money. Jesus, who knew people's hearts, cautioned repeatedly against the snare of wanting to be rich. Later in this guide we'll look at his parable of the rich fool. In this study we'll look at Jesus' account of the rich man, who, like an Ebeneezer Scrooge, shut up his compassions toward the less fortunate.

1. Think about times in your life when you've battled with covetousness, poverty, dishonesty, selfishness, or hoarding. Share a specific difficulty you've had with money.

⌀ READ LUKE 16:19-31.

2. Proverbs 11:4 states that "wealth is worthless in the day of wrath." How was this true for the rich man? What is the only thing that will save you in the day of wrath?

3. What do the rich man's two requests tell you about him and his priorities? What do you learn about the reality of hell from this passage?

⌀ 4. To whom was Jesus telling this story? (See verse 14.) How did Abraham's second reply apply to them?

5. You may have heard people say that they would believe in God if he would do something spectacular to prove himself. What do you think about this

statement? What have you seen in your lifetime to justify your conviction?

6. Some people feel they are safe from God's wrath because they are just one among many sinners. Some people feel they are safe because they are beautiful or rich. What makes you feel secure? How will this help you escape condemnation?

⌒ READ PROVERBS 10:2-5,15-16,22.

7. What do these verses say about different ways of obtaining wealth? about God's provision?

✍ 8. What do you think verse 15 means? How do you see this manifested in life?

READ PROVERBS 11:1-4,7,18-29.

9. Verse 1 says a dishonest scale is an abomination to the Lord. What are some business practices today that seem to fit this category?

In what ways could verses 3-4 guard you from the temptation to be dishonest?

10. What are some examples of hopes that perish when wicked men die (verse 7)?

11. In what ways do generosity and stinginess affect a person's life, reputation, and family (verses 16-29)?

12. Proverbs 13:7 says, "One man pretends to be rich, yet has nothing; another pretends to be poor, yet has great wealth." What does this mean?

13. What are you investing your life in that will pass away? What are you investing in that will not pass away?

The Lamp of the Wicked

MATTHEW 25:1-13; SELECTIONS FROM PROVERBS 12 AND 13

illions of people who have immigrated to the United States have expressed the hope that the Statue of Liberty gave them when they sailed into New York harbor. "Give me your tired, your poor, your huddled masses yearning to breathe free," she promises.

Yet many Americans are no longer compassionate toward the tired and the poor. They may believe they are Christians, but their hardheartedness and evil words indicate otherwise. As Solomon repeatedly said, our actions reveal whether we have the True Light within our hearts. Although we are not saved by our good works, good works reveal a heart of saving faith. And if we are not saved, one day our lamp will be "snuffed out."

1. Describe a time when you were afraid of the dark. (This may be a childhood memory or a frightening experience that happened more recently.)

Read Matthew 25:1-13.

2. What happened in this parable?

3. How were the ten virgins alike? How were they different?

4. Why were the five virgins who didn't have oil surprised? How can you apply this parable to your life? (See also Matthew 7:21-23.)

5. If Jesus were to return today, would he find you wisely prepared or foolishly unready? How can a person make sure he or she is prepared for Jesus' return?

READ PROVERBS 12:3,11,14,19,28.

6. According to verses 11 and 14, what must we do for our lives to bear good things?

What can get in the way of our accomplishments (verse 11)? How might this relate to the parable of the ten virgins?

7. According to verses 3, 19, and 28, what will bring us immortality?

READ PROVERBS 13:1,9,13-16,18,20.

8. What similar thought is repeated in these verses?

Has your way ever been hard as a result of your unfaithfulness? If so, share your experience. (verse 15).

9. What truths are presented in verse 20? Have you seen these truths played out in your life or in the life of someone you know? Explain.

10. According to verse 9, the "lamp of the wicked is snuffed out." Remember what happened to the foolish virgins in Jesus' parable. What parallels do you see between this verse and the story of the ten virgins?

What parallels do you see between the foolish and the wicked in Proverbs 12?

11. In what ways do you see the "light of the righteous" shining brightly in the world today?

What can you do to allow God's light to shine through you?

A Wise Servant

MATTHEW 24:45-51; SELECTIONS FROM
PROVERBS 14 AND 15

In *The Prophet,* Frank Peretti writes about a man running for office who pretended to have a servant's heart but was driven by ego, lust, and the special interest groups who helped get him elected. Slick advertisements and a corrupt media made him look like a servant when, in truth, he was a fool. (Remember that a fool is a person who lives life without fear of or regard for God.)

It's an age-old problem. In 1648 a count wrote in despair to his son, "Dost thou not know, my son, with how little wisdom the world is governed?" As God's servants we have been given charge of managing the world. But how foolish we can be in our care of it! In this study the book of Proverbs shows us how we can be wise servants—and Jesus shows us the consequences if we rule as fools.

1. Has there ever been a time in your life when serving made you feel either pleased or ashamed? Why did you feel this way?

READ MATTHEW 24:45-51.

2. What attitude led to the downfall of the wicked servant?

✐ 3. What will the faithful and wise servant be found doing when the master returns (verse 45)?

What will happen to the wise servant when the master returns? What will happen to the wicked servant?

4. How does God reward faithfulness? What does this say about our attitude toward responsibility?

5. What are some specific ways that you can be faithful in your speech until Jesus returns? in your actions?

READ PROVERBS 14:1,14,23; 15:15-17.

6. Give an example that illustrates how a wise woman builds her home. How might a woman tear down her home? Is it possible to tear down your home by serving too much? How do you decide how much service is too much?

7. What is the simple message of Proverbs 14:11,14?

8. Sometimes being a faithful servant means living on a lower income. What consolation is there for those who choose a simpler lifestyle (15:15-17)? If you have had this experience, share something about it.

READ THE FOLLOWING VERSES.

Be sure you know the conditions of your flocks, give careful attention to your herds; for riches do not endure forever, and a crown is not secure for all generations. (Proverbs 27:23-24)

9. When these words were written, servants took care of other people's property. How would these verses apply in that situation?

10. What warnings do we find in these verses? What assurances?

11. In the following proverb, what determines who rules and who serves?

   Diligent hands will rule, but laziness ends in slave labor.
   (Proverbs 12:24)

   In what way could a servant actually have *more* honor than someone with higher status?

12. What does the following proverb tell us about the value of a skill that is well developed?

   Do you see a man skilled in his work? He will serve before kings; he will not serve before obscure men.
   (Proverbs 22:29)

What does this verse imply about our influence in
the world? Do you know someone of "servant"
status who greatly impacts the lives of those
around him or her? Why do you think this is so?

Spend time this week praying about the opportunities you may
have for making a difference in the world.

Trust in the Lord

JOHN 10:1-18,27; SELECTIONS FROM PROVERBS 16

erhaps God gave author Paul Little a premonition of his death. A few weeks before he was killed in an automobile accident, Paul said on a radio broadcast, "It could be that God will take me before what people consider to be my time. If that happens, the question that should be asked is not, 'Why?' but 'Is God good?' And we know God is good, for he so loved the world that he gave his only Son." After his death, Little's words consoled those who loved him.

Solomon said, "Blessed is he who trusts in the Lord" (Proverbs 16:20). Likewise, Jesus shows that he cares so much for us that he is willing to give his life for his sheep. We would be wise to trust this Shepherd who loves us and seeks our good.

1. Describe a time when it was difficult for you to trust the Lord, but you did anyway. What did you learn?

Read John 10:1-18,27.

2. Who do each of the following represent? List two or three things you notice about each one.

the good shepherd (verse 11)

the sheep (verse 4)

the hired hand (verse 12)

the wolf (verse 12)

other sheep "not of this sheep pen" (verse 16)

3. Why do the sheep trust the shepherd? How does that trust improve their lives?

4. In verses 3, 4, and 27, Jesus says his sheep hear and know his voice. On a moment-by-moment basis, how can you—or how do you—distinguish Jesus' voice amidst the clamor of the world around you? What other voices call to you?

5. Jesus is the Good Shepherd who lays down his life for the sheep. How does this truth encourage you to trust him when his way seems hard or strange? Give an example if you can.

Read Proverbs 16.

6. Which verses in this chapter tell you that God is in control? Which one(s) most encourage your heart to trust him?

7. Two elements are presented in verses 1 and 9: the planning of the human mind and the giving of wisdom from God. In what ways can these two levels of understanding work together?

8. Verse 3 is quoted frequently in Christian circles. How does this passage work in real life? Do you agree or disagree with it? Why?

9.   We can expect to have enemies as we live the Christian life. What does verse 7 mean? In what ways have you experienced the truth of these words?

10.   Pride causes us to trust in ourselves rather than in God. What warnings and exhortations do you find in verses 5 and 18-20?

11.   Meditate on verse 20. If you can, describe a particular area in your life that has changed for the better because you paid attention to the Word. How has trusting in the Lord brought you blessings?

12.   What do verses 2 and 25 tell us about ourselves?

Do these verses imply that we *intend* to go the wrong way or that we are not capable of knowing what is best? Explain your answer. Give examples from your own experience if you can.

Take time to be still before the Lord. In what specific areas is the Lord telling you to trust him? If you feel comfortable doing so, share your thoughts with the group. Pray for the members in your group, and check in with one another during the coming weeks.

The Lord Tests the Heart

MATTHEW 15:1-20; SELECTIONS FROM PROVERBS 17 AND 18

In Karen Mains's story *Tales of the Kingdom,* the people of the Kingdom must pass through the "Sacred Flames" to get to the King. The fire is painful for a moment, but upon entering the inner circle, a crippled girl straightens up, lovely and shining; an old woman becomes young and dazzlingly beautiful, and everyone can see a beggar for who he truly is: the King.

Solomon said, "The Lord tests the heart" (Proverbs 17:3). The fires of life and eventually the "Sacred Flames" will reveal what we truly are. Some people who were honored in this life will have nothing left after they have passed through the fire. And some who were despised will come forth shining as gold. With this perspective, Jesus' rebuke to the Pharisees in Matthew 15 is full of meaning.

1. Briefly describe a "fire" you have endured—either a small test or an intense trial.

What did this experience reveal to you about yourself?

READ MATTHEW 15:1-20.

2. According to verses 1-9, what seems to be important to the Pharisees? How did their priorities affect their lifestyles?

3. What did Jesus tell his disciples concerning the Pharisees (verses 10-14)?

4. What defiles a person? Why? (See verses 17-20.) Reflect on the words you've spoken during the last twenty-four hours. What kind of heart do they reveal?

5. The words we speak reveal what is in our hearts. Knowing this, what specific suggestions would you make to the person who wants to improve his or her language and reactions?

READ PROVERBS 17:3,17,22.

6. Gold and silver are purified by intense heat (verse 3). What are some ways God may try or test our hearts?

7. Describe the heart of a friend or brother according to verse 17. How can you demonstrate this kind of heart?

8. What connection is made between the heart and a person's well-being in verse 22? What examples can you give to illustrate both parts of this verse?

READ PROVERBS 17:20,27-28.

9. According to these verses, how is a person's speech related to his or her character?

READ PROVERBS 18:2,6-8,13-14,20-21.

10. These verses have to do with listening and speaking. What principles are presented here?

11. Why is a listening heart important in each of the following situations?

in a Bible discussion group

at home

in the workplace

when we are witnessing about our faith

when we pray

Make Psalm 19:14 your prayer this week.

Unfailing Love

LUKE 10:25-37; SELECTIONS FROM PROVERBS 19 AND 20

When we adopted our five-year-old daughter, Anne, from an orphanage in Seoul, South Korea, she was withdrawn and sullen. She had never experienced unfailing love.

I remember when Sarena, a six-year-old who had been praying for Anne, came to meet her. Sarena held out a teddy bear, which Anne took and threw to the ground. Sarena persisted, trying to coax Anne to go swing with her. Anne refused. Sarena gently said, "Anne, I just want to be your friend." Anne, not understanding English, scowled at Sarena. I will never forget Sarena's response. She turned to me and said, "Mrs. Brestin, I don't care how long it takes. I'm just going to keep on being nice to Anne. One day we are going to be best friends."

God used a six-year-old to restore my daughter. Solomon tells us this kind of love is very rare, and Jesus shows us that the truly spiritual people are the ones who show unfailing love.

1. Give an example of someone who showed you unfailing love.

READ LUKE 10:25-37.

2. Describe the actions of the priest and the Levite in this parable. Why would we expect them to show unfailing love? Why do you think they didn't?

3. Have you ever behaved like the priest and the Levite? Why did your love fail, and how can you avoid repeating this sin?

4. Describe the actions of the good Samaritan. Why is he such a good example of unfailing love?

5. Unfailing love is very rare, but it exists. From Jesus' command in verse 37, how do we know that it is possible for us to show unfailing love to others?

What does this parable say to you in your present life situation?

READ PROVERBS 19:2,4,6-7,22.

6. Who in the parable we just studied is an example of the proverb in verse 2?

Describe a time in your life when your haste or religious zeal got in the way of your ability to show real love.

7. Faithful friends are very rare. How is that demonstrated by the truths in verses 4 and 6-7?

8. According to verse 22, each of us desires unfailing love from others. List some qualities that demonstrate this kind of love.

READ PROVERBS 20:6,28.

9. What does verse 6 say about unfailing love? In what ways have you seen this demonstrated in life?

10. How can love and faithfulness keep a king safe (verse 28)?

What do we usually think of as protection for political authorities?

Read Proverbs 20:3,22 and the following verses.

Hatred stirs up dissension, but love covers over all wrongs. (Proverbs 10:12)

He who covers over an offense promotes love, but whoever repeats the matter separates close friends. (Proverbs 17:9)

11. Studies show that the reason we are often most hurt and disappointed in quarrels with friends or family members is because there seemed to be a lack of love. What wisdom about quarrels is offered by these verses?

12. When a friend or family member lets you down, what response do you think is most pleasing to God, based on the verses in this study?

Spend time this week meditating on what "unfailing" love means.

Thorns and Snares

LUKE 8:4-15; SELECTIONS FROM PROVERBS 21 AND 22

In his poem "The Rose," Robert Herrick lamented that thorns don't always include roses, but a rose always has a thorn. Mr. Herrick forgot one man who was born without the ugliness of the thorns of sin: Jesus Christ. Isn't it ironic that he wore a crown of thorns when he redeemed us?

Thorns symbolize things that are hurtful, spiteful, ugly, or dangerous. Unfortunately, life is full of them! The book of Proverbs shows that the wicked stumble over thorns all along their life path. And Jesus tells us we must beware of thorns that can choke out the seed of his Word. We who follow him must be sure that our lives are open, not to the disruptive thorns of modern-day life, but to the Rose of Sharon.

1. What are some of the "thorns" or "snares" in your life?

READ LUKE 8:4-15.

2. How did each of the following four soils respond initially to God's Word? How did each of them respond on a long-term basis, and why?

the path (verses 5,12)

the rocky soil (verses 6,13)

the thorny soil (verses 7,14)

the good soil (verses 8,15)

3. According to verse 13, what three things do the thorns represent? Do any of these thorns threaten to choke you? Explain.

4. What kind of "soil" are you? How can you better cultivate your soil?

READ PROVERBS 21:2-3.

5. In Solomon's day, believers sometimes deceived themselves into thinking they were obeying God as long as they were bringing him sacrifices. Today, believers make a similar mistake when they think that as long as they are busy with "church things," they are obeying God. Meditate on Proverbs 21:2-3. What is God saying to you?

READ PROVERBS 21:16 AND THE FOLLOWING VERSE.

A discerning man keeps wisdom in view, but a fool's eyes wander to the ends of the earth. (Proverbs 17:24)

6. In Jesus' explanation of the parable of the sower, he described the person in whose life God's Word is "snatched away" by the devil. According to these verses, how do we contribute to our own under-standing—or lack of it?

READ PROVERBS 21:6,17,25-26.

7. Jesus taught that fruitfulness in a person's life can be choked out by "life's worries, riches, and pleasures." What insights do the verses in Proverbs 21 offer concerning such distractions?

READ PROVERBS 22:5-6.

8. Meditate on verse 5. Ask the Lord to show you any thorns or snares that are choking out the vitality in your spiritual life and the changes he would have you make. List the thorns or snares the Lord has shown you and the changes he is asking you to make.

9.   Proverbs 22:6 is a well-known verse. What are some specific ways to train up a child in the way he or she should go?

How will good training protect young people from thorns?

Read Proverbs 22:24-25.

10.   A recurring theme in Proverbs is that close friends who have bad habits can be a snare to us. How has the truth of this passage been demonstrated to you?

Read the following verses.

The righteous will never be uprooted, but the wicked will not remain in the land. (Proverbs 10:30)

If you falter in times of trouble, how small is your strength! (Proverbs 24:10)

11. Jesus also talked about a person who has no spiritual roots. What do these proverbs say about people who have developed roots in their character and lifestyle?

READ PROVERBS 22:17-21 AND THE VERSE BELOW.

He who obeys instructions guards his life, but he who is contemptuous of his ways will die. (Proverbs 19:16)

12. According to these verses, how can our lives become "rooted"?

Find a prayer partner who will hold you accountable and help you cultivate your spiritual soil over the next month. Make plans to pray with him or her at least once a week.

He Who Weighs the Heart

MATTHEW 18:23-35; SELECTIONS
FROM PROVERBS 23 AND 24

In her book *The Missing Piece,* Lee Ezell tells how, as a pregnant teenager, she had to decide between aborting her child or giving her child life. Lee chose life and gave birth to the only child she would ever conceive—a beautiful daughter. Lee makes an important observation about the hard choices we must make in life:

> I've found the things of God are often very hard to do at the beginning, but they are very easy and peaceful in the end. While the wrong choices are so easy to make at the beginning, they end up so complicated and full of difficulties and regrets later.

Often we teeter between good and evil. Our minds bang like a seesaw between the two. On which side will we add the weight?

1. Think about a recent choice you made between good and evil (something you said or read or

watched or did). Which way did you teeter? What thoughts came to your mind? What was the result?

READ MATTHEW 18:23-35.

2. In what ways is God like the "certain king"? For whom in this story do you feel the most sympathy? Why?

3. Why did the king forgive his servant? What is the central point of this parable?

✐ 4. When we are teetering between the choice to forgive
someone or to stay angry with him or her, what
warnings does this parable give us?

5. To what specific circumstance in your life can you
apply this parable?

Turn to Proverbs 23 and 24.

6. Imagine yourself teetering on the edge of a choice
between good and evil. What might be the temptation in each of the following passages? What is
God's message to you in that moment?

23:19-21

23:22-25

23:26-28

23:29-35

24:8-9

24:11-12

24:17-18

24:23-26

24:28-29

24:30-34

7. Which of the temptations in these passages is most likely to occur in your life? Summarize God's warning for that particular temptation and memorize it.

8. How does childhood training "by the rod" keep us from wickedness (23:13-14)? When do you think God would want a parent to spank, and in what manner?

Pray that God will grant you mercy for the times you have made the wrong choice and teach you to discern between good and evil.

A Place Among the Great

LUKE 14:7-11; SELECTIONS FROM PROVERBS 25 AND 26

Who of us, if we are honest with ourselves, does not want to be admired by others? And yet chasing honor is like chasing a butterfly—the harder you pursue, the higher it flies. Ironically, when you give up your butterfly chase and become absorbed in other things, it may come flitting back to you.

The search for honor springs from pride, which, according to C. S. Lewis, makes other sins "mere fleabites in comparison." This, Lewis said, is because "it was through Pride the devil became the devil: Pride leads to every other vice." If we want to become humble, we must first recognize how truly proud we are.

Once we recognize our pride, we can begin to turn from it, and with it, release our quest for a place among the great. Instead we must absorb ourselves in faithful and quiet service to God and to others. And it could be that when we serve with our whole hearts, God will bring honor back to us.

1. Solomon wrote, "Let another praise you, and not your own mouth; someone else, and not your own lips" (Proverbs 27:2). Have you ever wanted to tell

someone about your accomplishments? What was
that like? How do you feel when others tell you
about their accomplishments?

READ LUKE 14:7-11.

2. What warnings do you find in this passage?

3. What prompted Jesus to give these instructions?

What underlying human trait is revealed here?

4. Look carefully at verse 11. How was Jesus an
    example of humility? Give specific illustrations.

Read Proverbs 25:6-7,14,27 and the following verses.

Pride goes before destruction, a haughty spirit before a fall. (Proverbs 16:18)

Before his downfall a man's heart is proud, but humility comes before honor. (Proverbs 18:12)

A man's pride brings him low, but a man of lowly spirit gains honor. (Proverbs 29:23)

5. How do these verses point to the lesson of Jesus' parable?

When have you seen this principle at work? Give an example if you can.

6. Imagine that you feel you have a gift that other people have not recognized. You desire to sing a solo or lead a Bible study or be the pitcher on the

softball team. How do you think the Lord would have you apply the passages you just read?

Read Proverbs 25:8-10 and the following verses.

A perverse man stirs up dissension, and a gossip separates close friends. (Proverbs 16:28)

A gossip betrays a confidence; so avoid a man who talks too much. (Proverbs 20:19)

7. What is the relationship between a desire to "exalt oneself" and gossip? How, according to these three passages, can gossip boomerang and lower you in your friends' eyes?

Read Proverbs 25:14,17,23,28.

8. Thinking too highly of ourselves can sometimes hurt other people. How could this be the case in these verses?

Which of these verses speaks to you most personally?
Why?

9. According to Proverbs 25:20, what response is
    not helpful to those in grief? Why do you think
    this is so?

Read Proverbs 26:1-11.

10. A recurring theme throughout Proverbs is the fool,
    the person who lives life without regard for God.
    What do you learn about the fool in this passage?

11. Another definition of arrogance is "being wise in [your] own eyes." What do you learn about this in Proverbs 26:12 and 16? How could you avoid this pitfall?

READ PROVERBS 26:17-22.

12. Why are proud people often quarrelsome and gossipy?

13. What are some ways you can put the concept of humility to work in your workplace? in your church or study group? at your social gatherings?

He Who Chases Fantasies

LUKE 12:13-34; SELECTIONS FROM PROVERBS 27 AND 28

R emember the game of Monopoly? The object of the game is to buy up property and accumulate money, eventually monopolizing the available wealth.

It's hard to live in today's world without being seduced by the lure of materialism. Buying, owning, upscaling, and expanding consume our energies.

The disease of materialism has infected the church, too. The heresy of "prosperity theology" links God's blessings to material gain, promising that a faith-filled person can expect to be healthy and prosperous.

Jesus' parables and Solomon's proverbs have some strong teaching for the person who chases material wealth for selfish gain.

1. What are some fantasies you have chased? What are some ways you are endeavoring to become rich toward God?

✒ Read Luke 12:13-21.

2. Briefly describe the incident that led to this parable (verses 13-15). What does Jesus' warning mean to you in your present life circumstances?

3. What fantasy did the rich fool chase?

4. How might he have used his obvious talent for business to become rich toward God instead?

READ LUKE 12:22-34.

5. List the key lessons Jesus wants us to understand and obey.

6. Discuss the assurances Jesus gives in verses 31-32. What has the Father given us?

What do these assurances mean to you?

READ PROVERBS 27:1,12,20,23-24; 28:19.

7. According to verse 1, why should we never boast about the future? What are some ways to qualify any statement concerning our future plans?

8. The Bible does not tell us we should not make plans, but rather that we should realize that all plans are subject to the will of God. In fact, the person who chases fantasies often fails to plan ahead realistically and suffers for it. How this truth is illustrated in these verses?

9. What does Proverbs 27:20 say? In what area(s) of your life is God telling you to be satisfied?

Read Proverbs 27:6,9,17.

10. What do these proverbs tell you about the value of true friends?

Using these verses as a guide, list some ways friends might help one another develop a godly perspective about money.

Read Proverbs 28:6,11,14 and the following verses.

One man pretends to be rich, yet has nothing; another pretends to be poor, yet has great wealth. (Proverbs 13:7)

Of what use is money in the hand of a fool, since he has no desire to get wisdom? (Proverbs 17:16)

11. What do you learn about true riches from these proverbs? How could you apply this understanding to your life?

Have you ever seen Proverbs 28:11 illustrated? If so, explain.

✑ 12.   How does Proverbs 28:14 relate to Jesus' parable of the rich fool?

READ PROVERBS 28:20,22,25,27.

13.   What warnings do you find in these verses?

Which verses "hit home" for you especially? What will you do to apply what God has shown you?

When the Righteous Thrive

MATTHEW 5:13-16; SELECTIONS FROM PROVERBS 29 AND 30

t only takes a spark to get a fire going." A believer who is sensitive to God can make an enormous difference in his or her home, church, community, and nation.

This theme in Proverbs is repeated in the Sermon on the Mount. What a difference light can make in the darkness! But light is of no help if it is hidden under a bushel. And oh the change a little salt can make! But if salt has lost its saltiness, what good is it? Spiritual insensitivity makes our lives worthless.

Sensitivity to God brings continual refreshment and revival in our hearts, enabling us to thrive and make a difference in our world.

1. What are some ways you can tell when your spiritual life is blooming? What are some ways you can tell when you are going through a dry time?

READ MATTHEW 5:13-16.

2. Jesus said, "You are the light of the world." What did he mean?

3. Salt enhances flavor, creates thirst, and slows down the process of decay. How can believers be like this?

4. What did Jesus say about salt that has lost its saltiness?

What would a Christian who has lost his or her distinctive holiness be like?

5. List one or two convictions that God has given you about how to approach your life. What could you do, specifically, to "salt" our decaying world with these convictions?

READ PROVERBS 29:2,4,7,12,14,16,18.

6. Based on this passage, list the ways that righteousness and wickedness affect a nation.

Righteousness   *Wickedness*

7. Give examples from your own experience and observation of how these principles work out in everyday life.

🖋 8.   Here are two other versions of 29:18:

Where there is no vision, the people perish; but he that keepeth the law, happy is he. (KJV)

A nation without God's guidance is a nation without order. Happy are those who keep God's law! (TEV)

Explain how the truth of this verse is evidenced in the world today.

READ PROVERBS 30:5-14.

9.   On the basis of these verses, what warnings could Agur have given God's people so that they would retain their saltiness?

10.   Have you ever prayed a prayer like Agur's in Proverbs 30:8-9? What prayer might you pray for yourself that is similar to Agur's?

READ PROVERBS 30:18-19,25-31.

11. One way to retain saltiness in your life is to allow creation to fill you with a sense of awe for its Creator. What are some of the things that amazed Agur in these verses? Why did he find them amazing?

    What have you seen today that fills you with a sense of awe for the greatness of your Creator?

12. If you continually embrace the attitude of Agur, what impact might this have on your corner of the world?

A Wife of Noble Character

PSALM 45; SELECTIONS FROM PROVERBS 31

According to Jewish custom, after a man and woman were betrothed to be married, the bridegroom went away to prepare a room for his bride in his father's house. During this time of waiting, the bride worked on her wedding gown (which symbolically represents character). Then, when everything was ready, the bridegroom returned in a great processional to take his bride home with him.

The 45th Psalm is a striking picture of a great king who lives in ivory palaces and is coming to wed his beautiful bride, who is "glorious" within her chamber. On a symbolic level, this is a description of Jesus and his bride. Who is the bride of Christ? It is every believing soul—all who have placed their trust in him. We belong to a God who woos, wins, and, one amazing day, will come back to wed us.

In the same way, the magnificent closing of the book of Proverbs speaks about a wife of noble character. On a literal level, she is an earthly wife, but on a symbolic level, she foreshadows the bride of Christ, who, because she has practiced the prevailing truths of Proverbs, thrills the King with her beauty. Like the bride in Psalm 45, she will be led to the King wearing embroidered garments, pleasing him with her beauty. And what makes her beautiful? Reverence, love, and trust in the Lord, which are the prevailing themes of proverbs and parables.

1. Jesus woos, wins, and one day is coming to wed you. What caused you to fall in love with Jesus? Was it his creation? His Word? His people? How did he win you?

Read Psalm 45.

2. The psalmist's heart is stirred by a noble theme, a picture or a parable of a future wedding. What descriptions of the majestic groom (who is actually Jesus) stand out to you (verses 2-8)? Why?

✐ 3. What is the bride told to do in verse 10? What do you think this means symbolically?

4. The bride's clothing is interwoven with gold that has been tested and purified. In what ways has your heart been tested and purified by the Lord?

5. A beautiful wife is praised by those she has impacted. In what ways do the closing verses of Psalm 45 and the closing verses of Proverbs 31 illustrate this?

⌁ **Read Proverbs 31:10-31.**

6. How can the church—as the bride of Christ—be like the woman of noble character?

7. List some of the tasks the woman of noble character does. What kinds of spiritual tasks might such a woman do? For example, what kinds of spiritual food and clothing might she provide for her family?

⌁ 8. What clues do you find in this passage for the reason and source of this woman's beauty?

9. Noble means "strong," referring particularly to strength of character. Why do you think the virtuous woman has the attitude described in verse 25? What reasons do those who belong to Christ have for not fearing the days to come?

10. How do those who know this woman feel about her (verses 11,28-29)?

How should those who come in contact with us as the bride of Christ—the church—feel about us?

11. What characteristics of the virtuous woman challenge you most?

12. How has this study of proverbs and parables helped you grow and bear fruit?

In what areas would you like to grow more?

Leader's Notes

STUDY 1: LET THE WISE LISTEN

Question 5. In the Bible *fear* has several meanings. In this instance the meaning is, literally, "fear" or "reverence" (*Young's Analytical Concordance to the Bible,* Grand Rapids: Eerdmans, 1970, p. 337). Often, though, fear means exactly that—even "terror" or "dread." In modern times, when people hate to think of having to answer to or "fear" anyone or anything beyond themselves, many of us have difficulty with "fearing" God. Part of accepting God's authority in our lives is accepting that there is reason to fear God—on many levels. In Luke 12:5, Jesus said it is wise to fear the One who "has power to throw you into hell."

STUDY 2: ALONG STRAIGHT PATHS

Question 10. Although it's easy to spend a lot of time bashing books and movies, this discussion should center on how and why we need to avoid certain paths. An alternate question might be, "What paths rejuvenate our minds, bodies, and spirits?"

STUDY 3: FIRE IN HIS LAP

Question 2. King David committed adultery with Bathsheba, she became pregnant, and David tried desperately to deceive her husband, Uriah. Failing, David sent Uriah to the battle front, where he was killed. (This story is found in 2 Samuel 11.) Scripture tells us that what David did displeased the Lord (2 Samuel 11:27). So the Lord sent his prophet Nathan to tell David this parable.

Question 4. The Lord knew that David "thought" with his heart. A story that would appeal to his emotions, rather than an outright accusation or reasoning that would appeal to his mind, would help him realize how wrong he had been. Moreover, David had been a shepherd as a young boy, so a story about a lamb would especially tug at his heart.

Question 7. Proverbs 5–7 form a unit that warns about immorality and encourages the preservation of the sanctity of sex in marriage. But adultery is also used in the Bible as an image for betraying our relationship with God and putting other things before him (see especially the book of Hosea). Emphasize this symbolic use of the adultery concept, because it applies to all of us.

Question 9. Inexperienced people often think it will not hurt them to listen to or look at a sinful situation, as long as they don't enter into it. A good question to ask ourselves is, "In what situations do I tend to rationalize playing with fire?"

STUDY 4: COME, EAT MY FOOD

Question 4. Those who have little in the world's eyes are often more receptive to the truth of God. Scripture repeatedly warns that material wealth can divert our attention from eternal treasures. Not only do such verses warn us to be content with what we have, but they prompt us to see "poor" people in a new light—as people who are often quite rich in the things of God.

Question 7. See 1 Kings 3:5-14 for background on Solomon's life.

Question 8. In Proverbs 9:1-5, Wisdom is preparing a feast for those who answer her call. Here, as well as in the following parable and in other places in Scripture, the call of God is represented by the image of a banquet or feast.

Study 5: Wealth Is Worthless

Note on Luke 16:19-31. Jesus does not call this a parable, and the fact that names are used may be evidence that this is a historical incident. In either case, the message in this passage is applicable to all of us.

Question 4. Just as the rich man's brothers would not listen to someone who came back from the dead any more than they had listened to Moses and the prophets, the Pharisees and other religious leaders of Jesus' day would need more than the miracle of the Resurrection to change their lives. We can see how, after Jesus rose from the dead, his prediction about their hardheartedness was true.

Note on the book of Proverbs. From this point on in Proverbs you will notice that chapters are much less thematic; a number of topics are covered in one chapter and are represented by a few verses or only one verse. For this reason passages in the studies will often include isolated verses from different parts of the chapter(s) and even some from completely different chapters that match the present subject of study.

Usually, selecting individual verses from various chapters is not wise when studying Scripture because this causes verses to be taken out of their larger contexts. Proverbs, however, is the only book of the Bible in which context is seldom an issue. These sayings were written, collected, and edited by kings (Solomon being a main source) and their scribes into short but powerful gleanings of wisdom.

Question 8. Wealth does in fact protect us from many things. For instance, today a wealthy person can afford better products, better medical care, better representation in a court of law, and even better police protection than a poor person. Verses in Proverbs such as 10:15 often say what is simply true in the world; notice this verse does not say that the situation should be like this, only that it is.

STUDY 6: THE LAMP OF THE WICKED

Question 2. In Matthew 24:42–25:1, Jesus introduced this parable by warning that he will come again suddenly, without notice. Evidently he used the parable of the virgins to further illustrate what he meant by lack of preparedness.

Question 3. The virgins were alike in their expectation of being able to attend the marriage feast (Matthew 25:1 and 11). They also looked alike on the surface. They were not alike in their preparedness (verses 2-4). Sadly, all of them thought they were prepared. Many people today who do not know Jesus as Savior and Lord feel self-confident about eternity. The foolish (and the wicked) do not embrace God in their hearts (Psalm 14:1), yet they feel they are right (Proverbs 12:15).

Question 5. This would be a good opportunity to distribute pamphlets, such as Campus Crusade's "The Four Spiritual Laws." It would also be a good time to review the basics of the Christian salvation message in the group, particularly if some people in the group have not heard a clear explanation before. A very "short form" of the good news is:

1. God is loving and holy. Every single person has not lived up to that holiness and in fact is unable to do so. We are all separated from God by our own sinfulness (Romans 3:23).
2. God provided a way back to him by having Jesus, who was without sin, take the punishment for our sins when he died on the cross (Romans 3:24-26).
3. It is not enough to know this intellectually. We must respond in repentance and faith, placing our trust in Jesus as our Savior and Lord (Acts 26:20; Romans 10:9-10).

Question 6. "He who chases fantasies lacks judgment" (Proverbs 12:11). These words speak strongly to the human tendency to live in self-delusion. The virgins who were left out of the wedding feast had not paid enough attention to the realities of life; the person who daydreamed rather than worked his land neglected the practical realities of seed time and harvest. In the same way we find it easy to avoid spiritual realities, and the results can be devastating.

Study 7: A Wise Servant

Question 3. First Peter 5:2-4 tells us, "Be shepherds of God's flock that is under your care, serving as overseers—not because you must, but because you are willing, as God wants you to be; not greedy for money, but eager to serve; not lording it over those entrusted to you, but being examples to the flock. And when the Chief Shepherd appears, you will receive the crown of glory that will never fade away."

Study 8: Trust in the Lord

Question 2. The Good Shepherd is Jesus, the sheep are believers, the hired hand is a false teacher (he is interested in the fleece and fat of the sheep but not in the sheep themselves), the wolf is Satan, and other sheep are Gentiles.

Question 4. While doing research for my book *The Lifestyles of Christian Women,* I surveyed four thousand women and looked carefully at 150 surveys of women whose lifestyles were truly transformed. They stood apart from their peers in radical obedience. I found that these women had some interesting habits in common. Most of them drastically restricted their television watching, and all of them spent time, daily, in the Scriptures.

Question 7. If someone has a *Living Bible,* have that person read Kenneth Taylor's paraphrase of these verses, since he captures the two levels quite well. Proverbs 16:1 reads, "We can make our plans, but the final outcome is in God's hands." Verse 9 reads, "We should make plans—counting on God to direct us."

Question 8. The principle of this verse often seems not to be true, partly because human "commitment" is seldom true spiritual commitment, and partly because our idea of "success" is rarely the same as God's. Our commitment may be superficial—in words only; it may be partial, with selfish motives overtaking it; it may be lacking in plain hard work on our part. And while we usually view success in terms of financial security, human (even Christian) approval, and large numbers of participants, converts, etc., God measures success by quite different standards, and many of these standards aren't very obvious in human terms. It is our responsibility to trust and obey with whatever understanding we are given—and leave results to God.

STUDY 9: THE LORD TESTS THE HEART

Question 6. God certainly tests those who experience martyrdom or other persecution for their faith. But God tests our hearts in much more subtle ways every day. Eleanor Roosevelt said, "Women are like tea bags. You can't tell how strong they are until they get into hot water." Hot water could be a small trial like a traffic jam, a rude clerk, or a forgotten appointment!

STUDY 10: UNFAILING LOVE

Question 7. In *The Friendships of Women* I quoted a nurse who said, "A good warm friendship is like a good warm fire. It needs continual stoking." When you get your feelings hurt, you don't feel like stoking. You feel like laying down the poker. And the fire dies. You might ask yourself: "How would Jesus respond in a situation like this?"

STUDY 11: THORNS AND SNARES

Question 8. This would be a good time to pray for one another. If yours is a small care group (or a large care group that could be divided), share with one another about what the Lord has shown you personally. What areas in your life need to be pruned in order for you to be more fruitful? Pray for one another now and throughout the week. Follow up on answers to your prayers.

STUDY 12: HE WHO WEIGHS THE HEART

Question 3. The king forgave his servant because he was merciful. It may be helpful here to note the difference between mercy and grace. Mercy comes into play when a person deserves punishment and the one offended does not give him the penalty he deserves. God granted us mercy when he sent Jesus to die in our place. Grace enters a life when a person has been given *more* than he deserves. God's grace is what allows us to enjoy and participate in his heavenly kingdom forever.

Question 4. In Matthew 19 Jesus says it is hardness of heart that makes people unwilling to forgive. The Lord is angered by an unforgiving spirit. Never be hardhearted! "Be kind and compassionate to one another, forgiving each other, just as in Christ God forgave you" (Ephesians 4:32).

Question 8. In these days of prevalent child abuse, many people struggle with the repeated scriptural admonition to not "spare the rod." Christian child-rearing experts have made some helpful distinctions. Dr. James Dobson recommends discipline for willful disobedience rather than for childish mistakes. You might ask group members for an example of each. Dr. Larry Christenson says that a spanking should always be approached with loving regret rather than anger. You are spanking not out of anger but out of obedience to God because you want to help your child learn to choose what is right. You might ask, "What are some ways your child would sense that you have a loving spirit when you spank?" Some of the ways you demonstrate a loving spirit include remaining calm, making sure your child understands what he or she did that was wrong, embracing the child after the spanking, praying together, and supporting the child. You might want to ask "When does spanking become abusive?" Ephesians 6:4 and Colossians 3:21 can provide you with some insight.

STUDY 13: A PLACE AMONG THE GREAT

Question 6. If your group is struggling with the idea of a gifted person truly not being recognized, you might ask: "What would be some ways to let others know of your interest without violating the lesson of these passages?" Expressing an interest in contributing to church life through a service is not prideful in and of itself. When we have a servant's heart—showing faithfulness in small or large tasks without being boastful— we have fulfilled what Jesus asks of us. In fact, many other passages of Scripture urge us to use the gifts God has given us.

Question 9. Bring some vinegar to pour on a little baking soda so the group members can see it fizz up. Ask them if there have been times when glib or pat comments about their suffering have felt to them the way this chemical reaction looks.

Arrogance comes into play when we try to give advice about a situation that we cannot relate to. It is foolish to say, "I know what you're going through" unless you truly have gone through a similar experience. Sometimes the best encouragement to a hurting person is our silent but empathetic presence, or such simple statements as, "I'm so sorry—I wish I could say or do something to make you stop hurting." Or, "I don't understand why this happened, but I know that God hurts with you."

Question 10. There may be some confusion about Proverbs 26:5-7 because these verses seem to contradict each other. However, this simply points out the truth of Solomon's words "There is a time to be silent and a time to speak" (Ecclesiastes 3:7). Sometimes it is wiser not to engage in an argument with a fool, and sometimes a soft word can help him see the error of his ways. Ask the Holy Spirit to give you wisdom!

STUDY 14: HE WHO CHASES FANTASIES

Note on Luke 12:13-21. The rich fool is a perfect example of the "fool" mentioned throughout the book of Proverbs. He was a fool, not because he was lacking in intelligence, but because he lived his life without regard for God. Proverbs 28:26 says, "He who trusts in himself is a fool."

Question 7. James 4:13-16 says more on this subject, recommending that we should make our plans by saying, "If it is the Lord's will, we will live and do this or that."

Question 12. The foolish use of money goes on all around us. Our culture pays athletes and movie stars more than it pays those who teach our children. Our government pays exorbitant prices for goods, due to a flawed political system. Brainstorm ways in which we do not honor God's priorities with our money.

Study 15: When the Righteous Thrive

Question 8. Amos 8:11-12 is a relevant passage on this subject.

Study 16: A Wife of Noble Character

Question 2. Christ is the true champion of the church, and one day he will bring justice for those who have been persecuted and martyred. One day our eyes truly will see the glory of the coming of the King. Encourage group members to describe the pictures in verses 3-6. The King is indeed coming from ivory palaces, and his robes will have the sweet-smelling aroma of myrrh, the perfume associated with his sacrifice for his bride.

Question 3. Again and again throughout the proverbs and parables, we are told to listen! In order to be chaste and holy, the bride is to live a separated life. She must separate herself from the things in the world that could pull her down, even from her own people, if they are not following the ways of the Lord.

Note on Proverbs 31. In this study, try to compare "The Noble Wife" with the title "bride of Christ," the church. Like the wife of Proverbs 31, the church should be productive, giving to the needy and providing for her own. She should bring her husband, Jesus, honor; she should bring forth fruit; and her lamp should "not go out at night." See what other literal and figurative similarities you can find in this chapter.

Question 8. Clues for the source of this woman's beauty can be found in verses 26 (wisdom of the Lord) and 30 (fear of the Lord). Her fruitfulness provides an interesting contrast to some of the fruitless people we have seen in Proverbs.

Question 9. The woman's strength comes from her trust in the sovereignty of God. She can laugh joyfully about the days to come because she knows God is good, and he does all things well in his time.

Question 12. Allow time for these wrap-up questions. Perhaps you could go around the room and let each person give an answer to one of these questions.

What Should We Study Next

T o help your group answer that question, we've listed the
Fisherman studyguides by category so you can choose
your next study.

TOPICAL STUDIES

Angels by Vinita Hampton Wright

Becoming Women of Purpose by Ruth Haley Barton

Building Your House on the Lord: Marriage and Parenthood
by Steve and Dee Brestin

Discipleship: The Growing Christian's Lifestyle by James and
Martha Reapsome

*Doing Justice, Showing Mercy: Christian Actions in Today's
World* by Vinita Hampton Wright

Encouraging Others: Biblical Models for Caring by Lin
Johnson

The End Times: Discovering What the Bible Says
by E. Michael Rusten

Examining the Claims of Jesus by Dee Brestin

Friendship: Portraits in God's Family Album by Steve and
Dee Brestin

The Fruit of the Spirit: Growing in Christian Character
by Stuart Briscoe

Great Doctrines of the Bible by Stephen Board

Great Passages of the Bible by Carol Plueddemann

Great Prayers of the Bible by Carol Plueddemann

Growing Through Life's Challenges by James and Martha
  Reapsome

Guidance & God's Will by Tom and Joan Stark

Heart Renewal: Finding Spiritual Refreshment by Ruth
  Goring

Higher Ground: Steps Toward Christian Maturity by Steve
  and Dee Brestin

*Images of Redemption: God's Unfolding Plan Through the
  Bible* by Ruth Van Reken

Integrity: Character from the Inside Out by Ted Engstrom
  and Robert Larson

Lifestyle Priorities by John White

Marriage: Learning from Couples in Scripture by R. Paul
  and Gail Stevens

Miracles by Robbie Castleman

One Body, One Spirit: Building Relationships in the Church
  by Dale and Sandy Larsen

The Parables of Jesus by Gladys Hunt

Parenting with Purpose and Grace by Alice Fryling

Prayer: Discovering What the Bible Says by Timothy Jones
  and Jill Zook-Jones

The Prophets: God's Truth Tellers by Vinita Hampton Wright

Proverbs and Parables: God's Wisdom for Living by Dee
  Brestin

Satisfying Work: Christian Living from Nine to Five
  by R. Paul Stevens and Gerry Schoberg

Senior Saints: Growing Older in God's Family by James and
  Martha Reapsome

The Sermon on the Mount: The God Who Understands Me
  by Gladys Hunt

Spiritual Gifts by Karen Dockrey

Spiritual Hunger: Filling Your Deepest Longings by Jim and
    Carol Plueddemann

A Spiritual Legacy: Faith for the Next Generation by Chuck
    and Winnie Christensen

Spiritual Warfare by A. Scott Moreau

The Ten Commandments: God's Rules for Living by Stuart
    Briscoe

Ultimate Hope for Changing Times by Dale and Sandy
    Larsen

Who Is God? by David P. Seemuth

Who Is Jesus? In His Own Words by Ruth Van Reken

Who Is the Holy Spirit? by Barbara Knuckles and Ruth Van
    Reken

Wisdom for Today's Woman: Insights from Esther by Poppy
    Smith

Witnesses to All the World: God's Heart for the Nations
    by Jim and Carol Plueddemann

Women at Midlife: Embracing the Challenges by Jeanie
    Miley

Worship: Discovering What Scripture Says by Larry Sibley

BIBLE BOOK STUDIES

Genesis: Walking with God by Margaret Fromer and
    Sharrel Keyes

Exodus: God Our Deliverer by Dale and Sandy Larsen

Ruth: Relationships That Bring Life by Ruth Haley Barton

Ezra and Nehemiah: A Time to Rebuild by James Reapsome
(For Esther, see Topical Studies, *Wisdom for Today's Woman*)

Job: Trusting Through Trials by Ron Klug

Psalms: A Guide to Prayer and Praise by Ron Klug

Proverbs: Wisdom That Works by Vinita Hampton Wright

Ecclesiastes: A Time for Everything by Stephen Board

Song of Songs: A Dialogue of Intimacy by James Reapsome

Jeremiah: The Man and His Message by James Reapsome

Jonah, Habakkuk, and Malachi: Living Responsibly
    by Margaret Fromer and Sharrel Keyes

Matthew: People of the Kingdom by Larry Sibley

Mark: God in Action by Chuck and Winnie Christensen

Luke: Following Jesus by Sharrel Keyes

John: The Living Word by Whitney Kuniholm

Acts 1–12: God Moves in the Early Church by Chuck and
    Winnie Christensen

Acts 13–28, see *Paul* under Character Studies

Romans: The Christian Story by James Reapsome

1 Corinthians: Problems and Solutions in a Growing Church
    by Charles and Ann Hummel

Strengthened to Serve: 2 Corinthians by Jim and Carol
    Plueddemann

Galatians, Titus, and Philemon: Freedom in Christ
    by Whitney Kuniholm

Ephesians: Living in God's Household by Robert Baylis

Philippians: God's Guide to Joy by Ron Klug

Colossians: Focus on Christ by Luci Shaw

Letters to the Thessalonians by Margaret Fromer and
    Sharrel Keyes

Letters to Timothy: Discipleship in Action by Margaret
    Fromer and Sharrel Keyes

Hebrews: Foundations for Faith by Gladys Hunt

James: Faith in Action by Chuck and Winnie Christensen
1 and 2 Peter, Jude: Called for a Purpose by Steve and Dee
 Brestin
1, 2, and 3 John: How Should a Christian Live? by Dee
 Brestin
Revelation: The Lamb Who Is a Lion by Gladys Hunt

BIBLE CHARACTER STUDIES

Abraham: Model of Faith by James Reapsome
David: Man After God's Own Heart by Robbie Castleman
Elijah: Obedience in a Threatening World by Robbie
 Castleman
Great People of the Bible by Carol Plueddemann
King David: Trusting God for a Lifetime by Robbie
 Castleman
Men Like Us: Ordinary Men, Extraordinary God by Paul
 Heidebrecht and Ted Scheuermann
Moses: Encountering God by Greg Asimakoupoulos
Paul: Thirteenth Apostle (Acts 13–28) by Chuck and
 Winnie Christensen
Women Like Us: Wisdom for Today's Issues by Ruth Haley
 Barton
Women Who Achieved for God by Winnie Christensen
Women Who Believed God by Winnie Christensen